DP
books

First Printing 2023

Copyright © 2023

Table of content

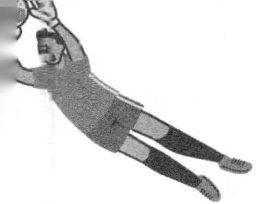

Table of content

Foreword

Hello, dear future professional footballer,

welcome to a world full of exciting football stories, specially written just for you! In this book, you will dive into thrilling adventures while learning many important things about teamwork, motivation, fairness, and, of course, football itself.

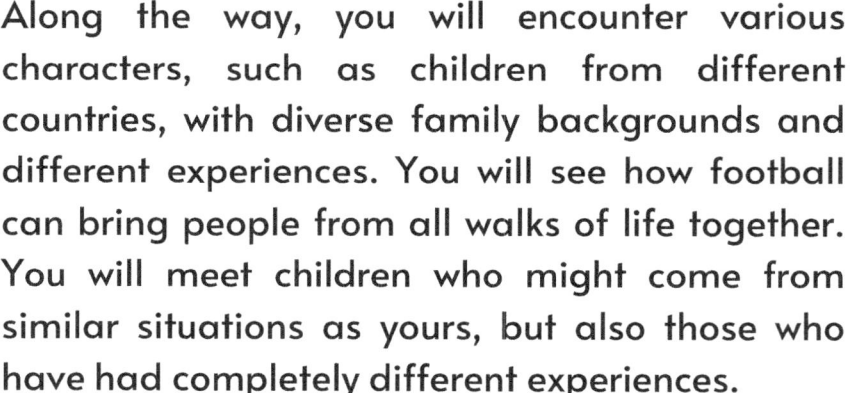

Along the way, you will encounter various characters, such as children from different countries, with diverse family backgrounds and different experiences. You will see how football can bring people from all walks of life together. You will meet children who might come from similar situations as yours, but also those who have had completely different experiences.

These stories narrate special moments on the football field. You will cheer along with the characters as they dribble, shoot, and score goals.

You will feel their joy as they participate in tournaments and compete against other teams. And you will experience how important it is for everyone to work together and give their best to be successful as a team.

But football is not just a game. In these stories, you will also learn a lot about important values. You will understand that team spirit and cooperation are crucial to overcome obstacles. You will see that fairness and respect towards your teammates and opponents are of great importance. These values will not only help you on the football field but also in your daily life.

You will also learn a lot about the game itself. You will learn how to control the ball, how to think strategically, and how important it is to have endurance and discipline.

And you will even learn about famous football legends who have shaped the sport. This book is not only filled with stories but also beautifully illustrated with images that will transport you into the world of football.

It will ignite your imagination and inspire you to pursue your own football dreams. You will see that football is a sport that brings people together and creates friendships.

So dive into this fascinating world of football and let yourself be captivated by the stories!

Have fun,

Your coach Dennis

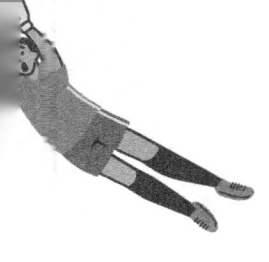

Marvin the lone wolf

Marvin was nine years old and preferred to be alone. While the other boys in his class engaged in sports and played games during recess, Marvin sat under the big oak tree and read. However, one afternoon, as he watched his classmates kicking the football back and forth on the field, his curiosity was piqued.

The boys were laughing and cheering each other on as they ran around and passed the ball to one another. Michael even sprinted with the ball at his feet, maneuvering through the others like slalom poles. When he scored a goal, they all jumped up and high-fived each other. Marvin noticed that he was smiling too. And he thought to himself, maybe it could be fun to play with them.

The next day during recess, Michael waved to Marvin. "Come on, play with us!" he called out. Marvin hesitated, feeling uncertain amidst so many children. But they kept urging him, so he slowly made his way onto the field. "Here, let me show you some passes," said Jake as he gently played the ball to Marvin.

At first, Marvin let it go through his legs, feeling shy. But the other boys encouraged him and gave him tips on foot positions and movements. Soon, he started playing passes back, and the whole group cheered. Marvin began to relax and enjoy the challenge of teamwork. From that day on, he played football during recess every day that week.

Before he knew it, a trial training session for the school's football team was announced. Marvin's new friends convinced him to come along.

Printed in Great Britain
by Amazon

19999553R00037

With their supportive tips, he completed some exercises for the coach. To his surprise, Marvin made it onto the team!

During their first big game, Marvin felt nervous on the sidelines in his jersey. But his teammates encouraged him and reminded him of everything they had practiced. Until the final minutes, their team was down by one goal. Then, the coach put Marvin in because he felt his speed could make a difference.

A few seconds before the end, the ball was passed to him, and he started running. Weaving through players, Marvin sprinted with all his might across the field. Just before the goal, he leaped over a slide tackle and landed with the ball a few meters in front of his feet. He took two steps and shot with full force - goal! His teammates piled on him in a huge celebration.

From that day on, Marvin never looked back when it came to football. He realized that being part of something bigger could bring even greater joy than doing things alone. Collaboration and friendship had shown him the special rewards of their own kind.

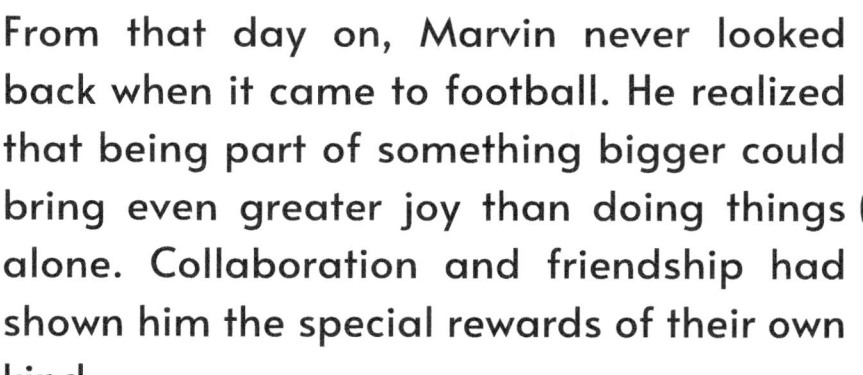

Jonas on a football journey

Jonas, in the third grade, was excited and a little nervous about his upcoming exchange to Italy. When his plane landed in Naples, he was picked up by the Rossi family, and warmly embraced by Signora Rossi. He finally got to meet his pen pal Nico and was served a plate of delicious pasta.

"You'll start school on Monday," said Mother Rossi. "But first, tomorrow you can meet some children your age at the park." The next day, Jonas followed his friend Nico, guided by the joyful sounds of laughter and the kicking of balls. In the park, the children were playing football. "Would you both like to join?" asked a boy named Marco. Jonas was thrilled and had a great time joining in a casual match.

He noticed that the Italian style of playing football focused more on defense than offense. After the game, Nico and Marco showed Jonas around the city, taking him to delicious pizza and tasty gelato. They practiced each other's languages and constantly had the ball at their feet. Jonas taught them English football songs while they taught him Italian songs.

On weekends, the three of them went together to cheer for their favorite teams – Marco and Nico were fans of Napoli, while Jonas' father was a fan of Roma. Jonas was impressed by the passion of the Neapolitan fans. His friends also told him about the history and rivalries between different football clubs. Jonas even heard stories about famous players like Moradano, and they showed him old videos highlighting his skills. He was inspired by Moradano's abilities and looked up to him as a role model.

Before he knew it, the school year was over. Jonas had become such good friends with his host family that he almost forgot he had ever lived elsewhere. Although he was sad to leave his friends, he boarded the plane with a deeper understanding and a greater love for football. Back home, Jonas could appreciate both the precise playing style of Italian players and the powerful style of English players. His journey abroad had expanded his horizons and shown him that football is a universal language. He would never forget this adventure.

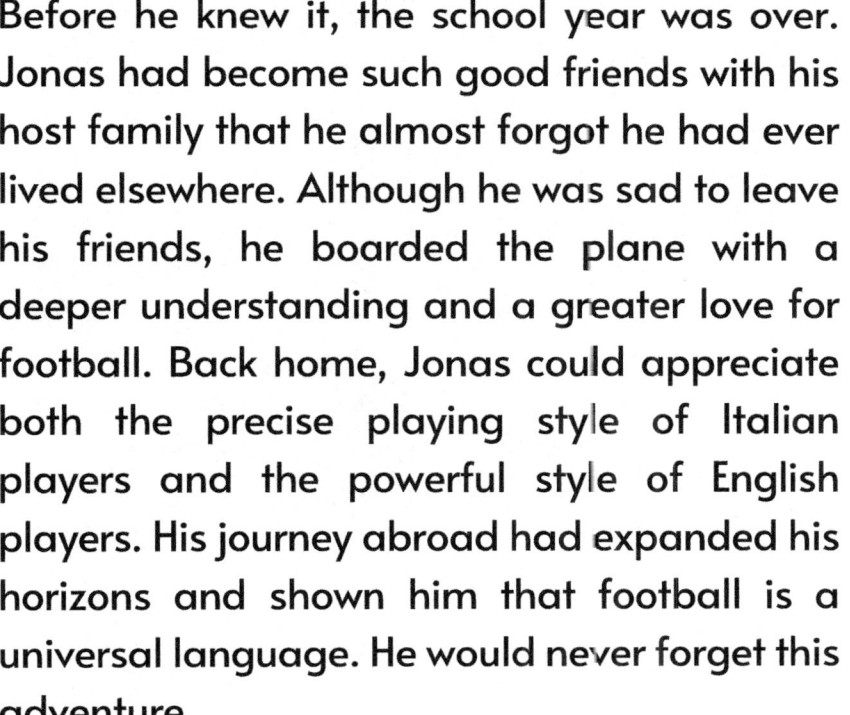

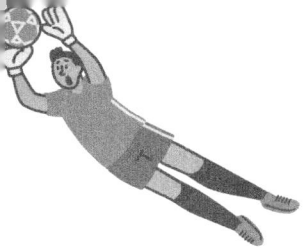

The lost ball

Carlos woke up full of excitement – today was the day of the big village tournament! But when he reached out to grab his ball, it was nowhere to be found. He searched frantically everywhere, but without success.

His father had given him that ball before he passed away from an illness. Carlos felt close to his dad when he played with it. Without the ball, Carlos felt lost. He decided to ask his friends for help in the search.

First, he went to Pedro's farm, where they often played. Although the fields yielded nothing, Carlos enjoyed feeding the chickens with Pedro. They joked about Pedro's rooster, who thought he was the real boss.

Afterwards, Carlos checked the stream near Maria and Julio's house. The twins were fishing, hoping for a good catch. But the water didn't reveal any clues about Carlos' ball. To cheer him up, Maria and Julio splashed around with Carlos in the water, making him laugh and momentarily forget his sadness.

As the sun began to sink, Carlos made a stop at old Manuel's place on the outskirts of town. Manuel was like a grandfather to all the children. "I think I saw a ball in the woods," he said. With a pounding heart, Carlos hurried into the dense forest.

He followed spiderwebs and broken branches along mysterious paths. Just as hope was fading, there it was - his ball, nestled among tree roots! Overjoyed, Carlos kicked it all the way back home.

Late in the evening, Carlos arrived at the tournament with renewed determination. However, his team was trailing by a wide margin nearing the end. The team was relieved that their best player was finally present and immediately substituted Carlos in. Shortly after, the captain passed the ball to Carlos, and a strange power surged through him – it was the strength and passion of his dad for the beautiful game!

Carlos now maneuvered around his opponents with full power, just like a professional, evading every tackle, and his team slowly closed the gap. Shortly before the end, thanks to Carlos, the score was actually tied.

Then came a through pass, right at Carlos' feet, who stood just a few meters away from the goal. He was calm and felt a warm, good sensation in his stomach. He knew what was about to happen. Carlos prepared himself and with a powerful shot that hit the upper left corner unstoppable, he scored the decisive goal just before the final whistle, leading his team to a jubilant victory. They came rushing towards him, throwing him up in the air in delight!

The spirit of his dad had given him wings to achieve victory for the village. Carlos had learned that true strength comes from within and is most powerful when shared with others.

Paul's big football game

Paul could hardly sleep before the big game. The next morning, his mother called the team for breakfast. "Eat well, you champions!" she said with a smile.

On the field, Paul's team did warm-up exercises. They had learned new tactics that were working well. John was in a particularly good mood and scored many goals during practice. Paul felt confident.

The game started with the referee's whistle. Paul's team had control of the ball from the beginning. In the 15th minute, John dribbled past three defenders and shot the ball into the goal - 1-0! Everyone cheered.

But then, the opposing team fought back and tested the defense. However, goalkeeper Sam made great saves and maintained the lead until halftime. After a short break, the game resumed.

In the middle of the second half, the other team scored a goal due to an unfortunate deflection. And then, with only 10 minutes left, they took the lead with a swift attack. Paul's team was surprised and disappointed.

The coach called for a timeout and said, "Don't hang your heads! One goal, and we can still win this game. Show them what you're made of!" Everyone was motivated and gathered together.

After another great save, goalkeeper Sam had the ball and threw it far to Paul. He dribbled past two defenders and shot the ball into the goal - equalizer! Everyone cheered and was filled with excitement!

The game became more and more intense as both teams gave their best. But Paul's team's defense, led by captain Sam, held strong.

In the final seconds, Paul intercepted a pass and played a precise through ball right into John's path. Without hesitation, John swiftly shot the ball into the lower right corner. The rivals' goalkeeper could only watch as the ball hit the back of the net and started to ripple.

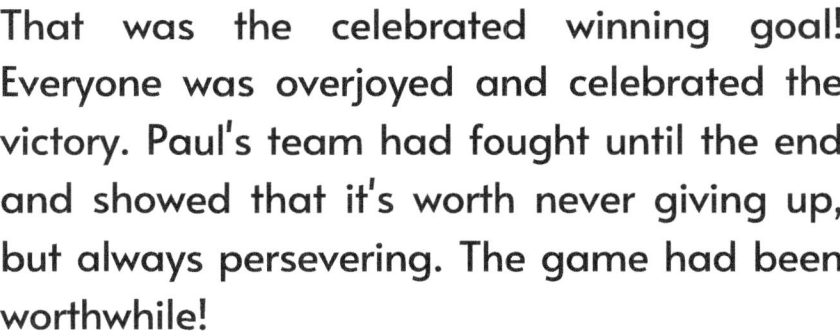

That was the celebrated winning goal! Everyone was overjoyed and celebrated the victory. Paul's team had fought until the end and showed that it's worth never giving up, but always persevering. The game had been worthwhile!

Max, the too small goalkeeper

Max loved playing in goal, but at only 9 years old, he was the smallest on the team. In their first game, the opposing forwards quickly learned to shoot the ball over his head and into the goal.

By halftime, Max had conceded 5 goals, while his teammates shouted at him, blaming him for the goals. Sad and with his head down, he wished he could prove them wrong.

After the game, Max frustratedly stomped around on the sidewalk, kicking stones. That was when the old man, Roberto, approached him. "Don't let your size discourage you, young man," he said.

Roberto himself had been a goalkeeper in the past and began telling Max about angles, positioning, and reading the game. "With practice, you can control the penalty area through skill, not size!"

He invited Max to train in his backyard. There, Roberto taught Max how to read the movements of the forwards. They then worked on footwork, with Max skillfully maneuvering around cones.

For diving practice, Roberto hung an old sock on a tree. Max lunged and stretched with all his might, trying to knock the sock away each time

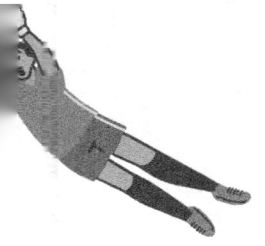

Weeks passed with this intense training. Max's reflexes and anticipation sharpened day by day. Finally, the next game arrived. And indeed, the forwards attempted to shoot the ball over him and into the goal early on. But Max had done his homework - he timed his jumps perfectly and was able to deflect the ball over the crossbar every time!

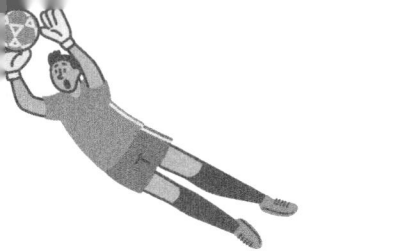

His defense held strong as Max commanded his penalty area. In the second half, an opposing forward charged towards the goal. In the last moment, Max somehow threw his entire body across the line to smother the shot!

The forwards had been accurate twice before, and his defense held as best as possible, while Max cleverly controlled the penalty area.

Throughout the game, Max executed several heroic saves, thwarting the opposing team's attacks with confidence. Then, in the second half, another opposing forward stormed towards the goal. In the final moment, Max fearlessly threw himself with his whole body in front of him to prevent the shot.

In return, Max threw the ball far ahead, right at the feet of his forward, who once again found the back of the net. The final whistle sounded, and Max's team won 3-0. His jubilant teammates surrounded him, and even the coach was impressed.

Roberto watched proudly from the stands, seeing the little goalkeeper he had always believed in. Max had proven that even the smallest players can turn weaknesses into strengths when they work hard. Because between the goalposts, it's not about size but about skill, bravery, and heart.

Leo and the special camp

Leo was a nine-year-old boy who loved football. He had always dreamed of attending a football camp where he could play with other children and learn new techniques. One day, he heard about a very special football camp that brought children from all over the world together. Leo could hardly believe his luck and immediately signed up.

Leo was excited as he went to the football camp but also felt a little nervous. Coming from an affluent family in Europe, he wasn't exactly sure what to expect.

When Leo arrived at the camp on the first day, he was thrilled by the number of children who shared his love for football.

The camp's coaches were experienced former professional players from around the world who taught the children how to shoot, dribble, and defend correctly. Leo was particularly excited because he could learn from some of the best players in the world. There was a coach named Diego who had previously played for the Portuguese national team and now passed on his football knowledge to the children.

During the camp, the children played in various training formats every day, both in teams and individually. Leo was amazed by the high level of the players. There were some children who were especially talented and played with incredible speed and precision. Leo was fascinated by their abilities and tried to learn from them, observing and picking up a few things.

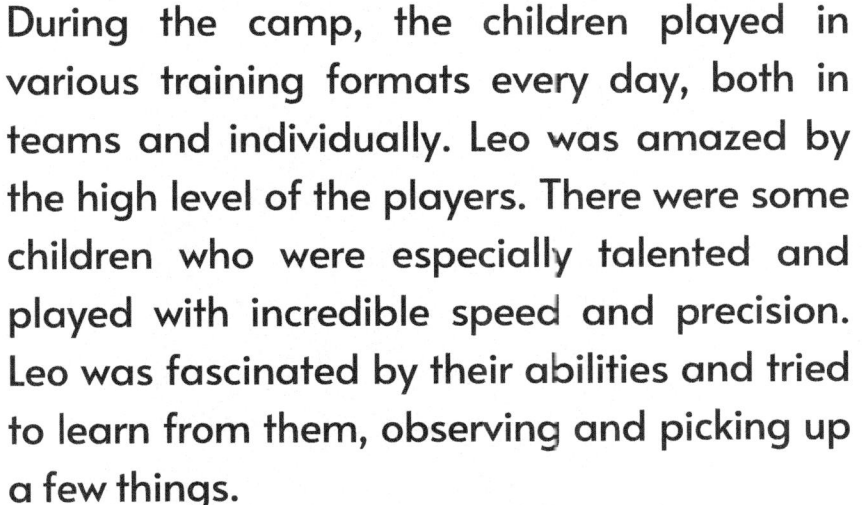

There were children from different countries such as Brazil, Spain, Japan, and many others. The camp was a vibrant place filled with energy and anticipation.

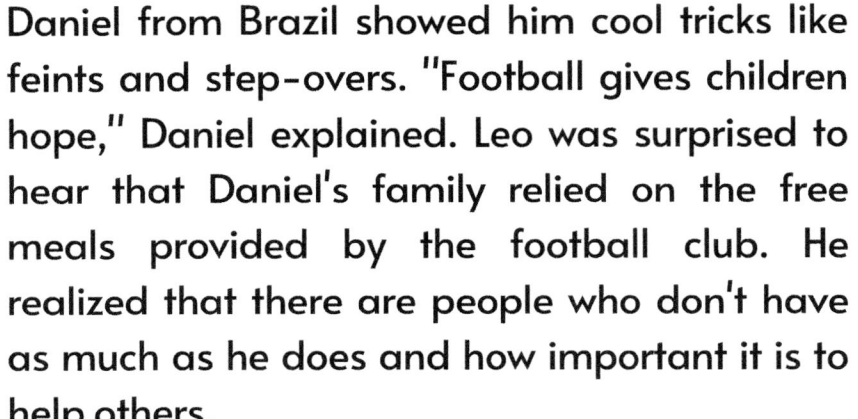

Daniel from Brazil showed him cool tricks like feints and step-overs. "Football gives children hope," Daniel explained. Leo was surprised to hear that Daniel's family relied on the free meals provided by the football club. He realized that there are people who don't have as much as he does and how important it is to help others.

Leo also befriended Afrat, a boy from Morocco. Afrat showed him photos of his village where there was no running water. The children had to walk long distances to fetch water, and going to school was difficult. "The football camp is changing our lives," he told Leo. "Now I can go to school and learn." Leo felt the strong will and determination in Afrat to make something out of his life and do his best despite the challenging circumstances.

Although the camp was competitive, the emphasis was not solely on winning. The coaches stressed the importance of teamwork, fair play, and respect. Each team had a colorful mix of players from different countries, and Leo loved how well they worked together and supported each other.

Leo also had the opportunity to improve his own skills. The coaches provided him with individual tips and advice that helped him enhance his game. He learned how to better control the ball, think strategically, and the importance of never giving up.

Additionally, the camp offered other activities. They painted, created crafts, and shared stories about football and friendship. Leo enjoyed this aspect as it allowed him to learn more about the cultures of the other children

What Leo loved the most was the diversity of people he met. He had friends from different countries and learned a lot about their languages, customs, and traditions.

Leo noticed that the best players in the camp were not only talented but also showed team spirit. They helped other children and encouraged them when they made mistakes. Leo desperately wanted to be such a player himself. He realized that football is more than just a game—it is meant to forge friendships, unite cultures worldwide, and have fun together.

During the camp, Leo began to brainstorm ideas on how he could help his new friends. He knew he had a privilege that many other children didn't have, and he wanted to give back. Leo started collecting donations by asking his family and friends for support.

With the possible money, he could buy water filters for Afrat's village, provide enough food for Daniel's family in Brazil, or obtain school materials for children in other countries. Leo promised his new friends that he would not forget them and that he would continue  working to help them.

After the camp, Leo stayed in touch with his friends. He regularly sent letters and packages with things they needed. He encouraged them to be diligent in school and to pursue their dreams.

32

In the football camp, Leo found not only an opportunity to improve his skills but also a new perspective on the world. Leo was grateful for the experiences he had in the camp and looked forward to continuing to support his new friends and staying in touch with them even after the camp.

Leo was proud of how far he and his friends had come. They had learned that football is not just a game but something that unites us all. Leo had realized that it doesn't matter where you come from, what language you speak, or how much money you have. What matters is that everyone has the power to do something good and bring joy to others.

The lonely football island

Once upon a time, there was a boy named Tim who embarked on an exciting journey on a boat. However, suddenly, the boat got caught in a violent storm and capsized. Tim desperately clung to a piece of driftwood, praying that he would be washed ashore somewhere. After a while, he lost consciousness.

When Tim regained consciousness, he found himself on a solitary, sandy shore.

He looked around and could see figures moving slowly on the beach in the distance. Curiously, he approached and saw people of all ages who, like him, had been affected by a shipwreck.

An older man named Paul seemed to be in charge of the group, but everyone was stressed and worried as they had very little food and fresh water. The mood was low. Amidst all the misery, Tim discovered a muddy ball in the sand on the shore.

"Hey, I have an idea!" Tim exclaimed excitedly. "Let's have a football tournament! Maybe it will lift our spirits and help distract us." Paul laughed mockingly, but the curious eyes of the others gave Tim hope. He began to assign the survivors into mixed teams.

Tim divided the survivors into different mixed teams. There were two brothers named Jimmy and Sam who often argued but ultimately played well together. Additionally, there was Amira, a girl who was a fantastic striker and motivated her shy teammates.

As the games began, laughter and cheers filled the air. People started exchanging players, cheering on their friends, and learning new skills. Even the old Paul, who was initially skeptical, discovered his joy in the game.

Although the brothers Jimmy and Sam often argued, they played wonderfully together on the field. Amira, a skilled striker, motivated her shy teammates with a positive attitude and scored goal after goal for her team.

The final of the tournament was particularly thrilling. Amira's team faced Sam and Jimmy's team. It was a back-and-forth battle until Amira scored the decisive goal with an impressive shot, securing the victory for her team.

But in truth, everyone felt like winners because they had stuck together and survived as one big family.

From that day on, everyone on the island worked together to survive until rescue finally arrived. They had learned that unity and teamwork are important, even in difficult times. And all of this was thanks to Tim's brilliant idea of bringing people together through the wonderful game of football.

A missed penalty kick

Luca could hardly wait to go to football practice as usual! He loved playing with his friends Marco, Gianni, and Sami.

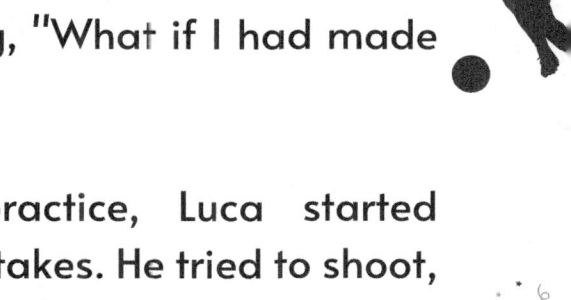

But during their big game last week, when Luca wanted to take the penalty kick to win, he missed. Their team lost, and Luca felt so sad. He kept thinking, "What if I had made the goal?"

During the next practice, Luca started making constant mistakes. He tried to shoot, but the ball just wouldn't go in. He also often stumbled over his own feet. Luca began to worry that everyone would be angry with him. His teammates tried to cheer him up, but nothing seemed to help.

Soon, Luca even started skipping training and was too anxious to face the team.

Before long, Luca stopped coming to practice altogether. He just wanted to hide in his room and stop playing football altogether.

Luca's friend Marco noticed that he seemed sad and missed him, so he started to worry. He went to Luca's house to check on him. "What's wrong, buddy?" Marco asked. Luca said, "I'm too scared to play after I lost the game for us."

"That's silly!" Marco exclaimed. "Everyone makes mistakes. We're still your friends, no matter what happens." On the way home, Marco soon came up with an idea to cheer Luca up.

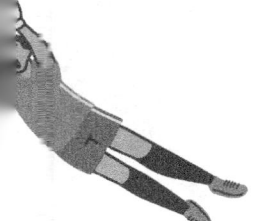

The next day, when Luca opened his front door, all of his teammates were there! When they arrived, Luca was shocked. "We're like a family, and you're our star striker." Finally, Luca began to smile again. "We enjoy having you on the team," Captain Gianna said. "Please come back to training with us, we need you!"

Luca started smiling again. This weekend, he and Marco went to the park to practice shooting goals. With each goal, Luca's self-confidence grew, and his old joy returned. In their next game, the team often passed the ball to Luca to help him succeed, and he was able to score goals.

Then, suddenly, a penalty was awarded, and Gianni took the ball and gave it to Luca. Luca didn't hesitate, he stepped up bravely and scored! His teammates embraced him in celebration, and Luca realized that with the support of friends and teammates, he could overcome anything—even missing a penalty—through the power of football.

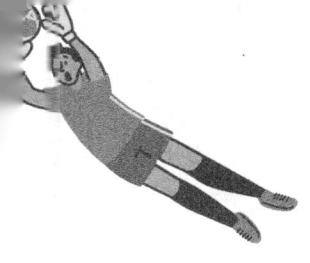

The language of football

Sepp was very excited about today's football training! He loved playing outdoors with his friends. On this day, he couldn't wait to go onto the field and have fun.

But when he arrived at the training, he saw a new boy from Asia. He was sitting all alone and looked a bit sad. Sepp wondered why the boy was so alone and decided to go up to him.

He decided to talk to the boy and used a translation app on his phone. "Hey, I'm Sepp. What's your name?" Sepp said kindly to the boy. The app slowly translated the words into Korean. The boy smiled widely and nodded.

He responded shyly, saying his name was Yam, that he was new to England, and not yet able to speak English very well.

Sepp wanted Yam to feel welcome, so he asked him, "Do you like football? We play a lot of football here, and it's always fun!" Yam was excited and nodded. He showed Sepp some cool ball tricks that Sepp had never seen before.

The other boys didn't include Yam in their warm-up games or passing drills. Sepp felt bad because Yam looked so sad because of it.

During a break, Sepp tried to communicate with Yam using hand gestures and a translation app. He learned that Yam loved playing as a striker but also missed his old team.

When the ball suddenly landed at Yam's feet, he showed the other boys some cool tricks with the ball that Sepp had never seen before.

Sepp was thrilled and wanted to help integrate Yam into his team. So he said to the other boys, "Hey, let Yam play with us! He's really good with the ball!" The other boys agreed and started including Yam in their games and drills.

Although the language barriers persisted, Yam's smiling eyes showed that he felt included.

After the training, Sepp invited Yam to his home to play video games, help him with translations, and teach him a few essential terms. During this time, Yam also shared stories about his home country, South Korea— a place that was very different but shared the same passion for football!

From that day on, Sepp and Yam became best friends. They supported each other during challenging training sessions and games. They helped each other with the language and learned from one another. Despite coming from different countries, their shared love for football brought them together, and their friendship grew stronger.

The moral of the story is that it doesn't matter where you come from or what language you speak; what matters is that you can have fun together and build friendships. Football is a universal language that can connect everyone, and it's important to be open and friendly to new people.

The great adopted talent

Ten-year-old Ivan woke up this morning and could hardly stay still due to excitement. Today was the big football selection day! Since his new mom and dad had adopted him, his greatest wish had been to play for the youth academy of his favorite team, Metro United.

When Ivan arrived at the football field, he saw that many other children were just as excited as he was. The coaches had prepared various exercises to test the children's skills. They had to dribble the ball through tight cones, make precise passes, and score amazing goals. Ivan found it challenging to concentrate at times because he remembered the time when he was alone in the orphanage.

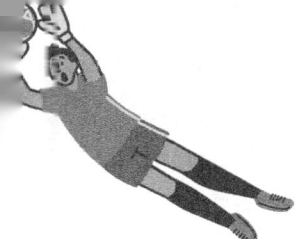

But Ivan wanted to prove that he was a great football player. So, he took a deep breath and gave it his all. He dribbled at top speed through the cones, making no mistakes and showing the coaches how well he could control the ball.

When it was his turn to shoot, he imagined the goal as a big gift. He hit the net perfectly and cheered with joy!

During the drills and small games, Ivan showcased his skills and completely lost his nervousness. He forgot about his past, accurately passed the ball to his teammates, and fought determinedly to win the ball from the opponents. The coaches could see how talented Ivan was, but deep down, he began to worry after a while because things were going so well. "What if the coaches think I'm not good enough?" he thought.

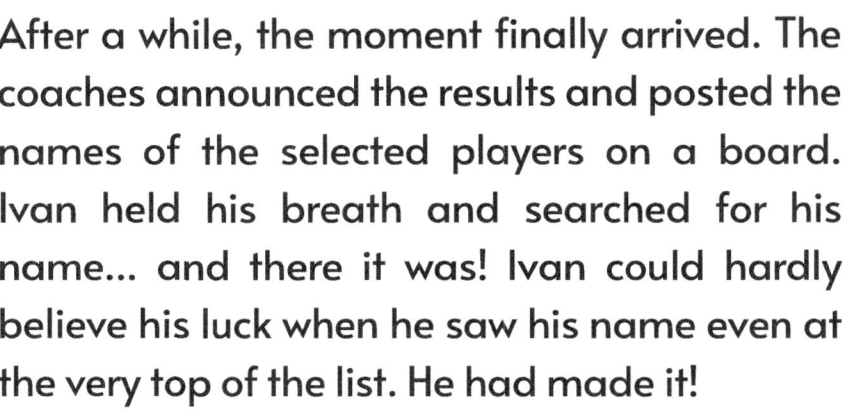

After a while, the moment finally arrived. The coaches announced the results and posted the names of the selected players on a board. Ivan held his breath and searched for his name... and there it was! Ivan could hardly believe his luck when he saw his name even at the very top of the list. He had made it!

A broad smile appeared on Ivan's face. He realized that all his hard work had paid off. He felt proud and knew that he was now part of a new football family. From now on, he would train and play with Metro United.

Ivan's dream had come true. Every time he kicked the ball, he thought of the joy and fun he experienced during the game, helping him process his past and the loneliness he had felt. And who knows, maybe one day he would even win the trophy with Metro United!

The moral of the story is that with hard work and passion, one can achieve their dreams. No matter where you come from or the difficulties you have faced, you can always find success if you believe in yourself enough.

The incredible tactical fox

Luis loved playing chess with his grandpa. Every time they moved the pieces across the board, Luis would think deeply and come up with new strategies to defeat his grandpa. Chess was like an exciting puzzle for him.

His friends thought that football was just about kicking the ball and running around. But Luis knew that there was so much more to the beautiful game! He understood that football could be like a chess game on the field, where one had to think cleverly and act strategically.

One day, during training with his football team, Luis had an idea. He began drawing formations in the mud to show his friends how the chess pieces move. They were curious and wanted to learn more.

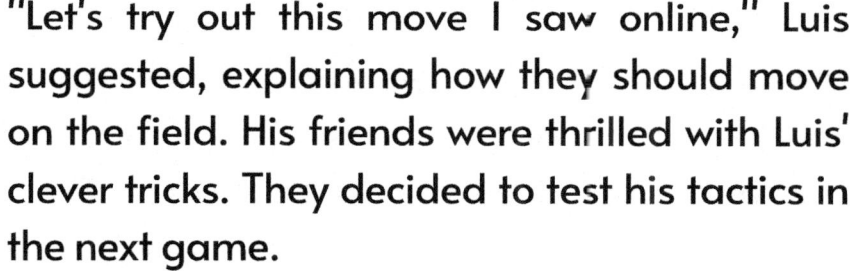

"Let's try out this move I saw online," Luis suggested, explaining how they should move on the field. His friends were thrilled with Luis' clever tricks. They decided to test his tactics in the next game.

In their first game using Luis' tactics, everything went smoothly! The team was always one step ahead, both in defense and in attack. The opponents were surprised by the clever moves and didn't know how to react. Luis' team won the game, and everyone was thrilled!

The news of Luis, the "tactics fox," spread like wildfire. Coaches and other teams took notice of him. Luis began studying video footage of famous football matches to learn even more tactics. He developed surprise attacks and special tricks to confuse the goalkeepers.

His friends were thrilled with the new moves and scored more goals than ever before. They not only had fun on the field but also learned the importance of thinking cleverly and working together as a team.

Finally, the team won the following six games and reached the final against the undefeated champions from a big city. Everyone thought they had no chance. But Luis had a secret weapon — a special strategy he had developed specifically for this game.

The final began, and Luis' team executed their clever moves. They were like a well-oiled machine, always one step ahead. When Luis' team performed a special play, the opponents were completely confused and didn't know how to react. The crowd cheered and cheered them on.

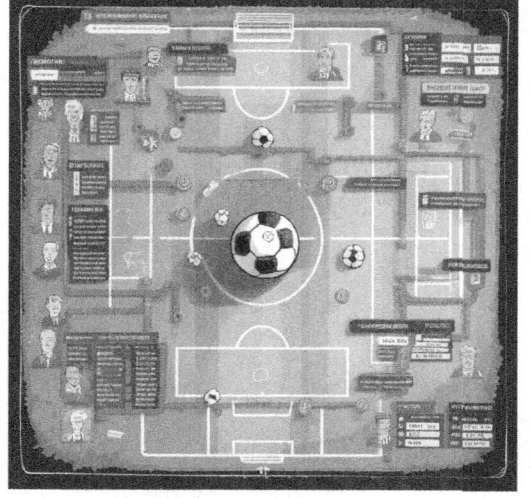

At the end of the game, Luis' team emerged as the winners! They had defeated the champions, and everyone was overjoyed. Luis was named the hero of the day and earned the nickname "Tactical Genius."

Luis proved that football is not just about running and kicking the ball, but that smart thinking and strategic action are equally important. His clever moves helped his team score more goals and win games. He showed that football can be like an exciting chess game where success comes from using your head and playing with teamwork.

A special football team

Liam didn't like making new friends because he had difficulty speaking due to a congenital speech impediment. During break time, he preferred to play alone with his ball.

One day, Liam saw a colorful poster: "Football Club for Special Children - for every child who overcomes challenges!" That caught his interest. He decided to go to the address to find out more.

Upon arrival, Liam saw children who had difficulty running or only had one arm. Others had Down syndrome and occasionally needed a hug. But all the children smiled when they kicked the ball and cheered each other on.

Liam was excited to be part of the special children's football club. In their first game, the children faced another team that laughed at them, didn't take them seriously, and defeated them easily with a score of 4-0.

It was a tough loss for the team. They were disappointed and felt defeated. Liam and the other children doubted themselves and wondered if they were good enough.

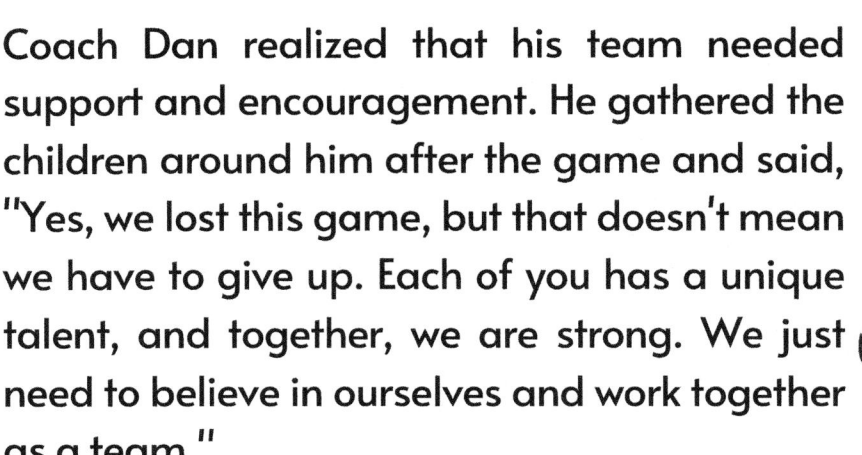

Coach Dan realized that his team needed support and encouragement. He gathered the children around him after the game and said, "Yes, we lost this game, but that doesn't mean we have to give up. Each of you has a unique talent, and together, we are strong. We just need to believe in ourselves and work together as a team."

The children listened attentively. They saw that Coach Dan truly believed in them and wanted to help them improve. They decided to train hard and support each other.

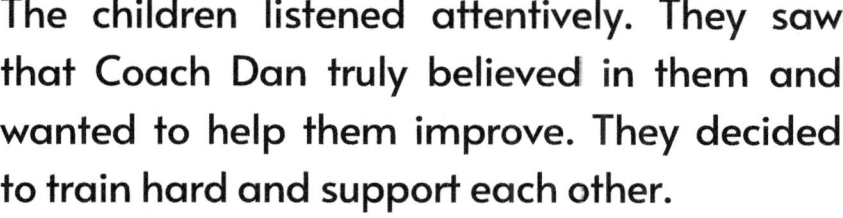

In the following weeks, they practiced intensively. They focused on their skills and worked on functioning better as a team. Coach Dan gave them tips and motivated them during every training session.

There were moments when the children felt frustrated and felt like they weren't making enough progress. But they didn't let it discourage them. They remembered their coach's words and that they were a family.

Over time, the children began to understand each other better. They knew where their teammates were on the field and how to work together best. They learned to rely on each other and support one another. Dan also taught them how to know where their teammate was without seeing them, so everyone could move better across the field.

When the team of special children started competing against other teams again, they showed impressive improvement. They still lost, but the score was now a close 1-2.

The children had learned that winning wasn't the most important thing. It was about sticking together as a team and giving their best. They had discovered their strengths and understood that they were unique as individuals and as a team.

Coach Dan was proud of his team. He saw how they had grown and how they supported each other. The special children's team had learned that true strength lies not only in victories but also in unity and friendship.

Then came the big rematch against the team they had lost 0-4 to and had been mocked by. The players from both teams were getting ready, and the opponents had already started laughing again before the kickoff. But as the referee started the game, the special children's football club showcased their skills.

The children from the team ran across the field like busy bees. They helped each other, passed the ball accurately, and scored amazing goals. Liam was particularly skilled at playing precise passes and putting his teammates in good positions.

The game was very close, and it was tied 2-2 until shortly before the end. The opponents were still confident of victory and laughed when the team didn't succeed at something. However, this would soon backfire on them.

The children didn't let themselves be discouraged. They worked together like a puzzle, showcasing great moves and supporting each other. With only a few seconds left on the clock, Liam had the ball. He sprinted towards the goal and unleashed an incredibly powerful shot. The ball flew into the top left corner of the net, and the entire field trembled with excitement!

The team of special children had won the game! They proved that as a team, you can achieve anything, no matter what challenges you face. True strength comes from within, and it's more important to be a good friend than to be physically perfect.

After the game, the children celebrated their victory. They were not just a team but also a family. Liam had found many new friends and was grateful for the support and fun he had with the special children's football club. They were already planning their next adventure and looking forward to continuing to play football together.

The ancient stadium

Robin loved playing with his ball every day in the large concrete buildings where he lived. One afternoon, as he walked towards the forest and explored an empty lot nearby, he discovered an old and dilapidated structure hidden behind a couple of trees at the edge of the woods, overgrown with vines and weeds. He found a gap and managed to enter the structure. Robin was amazed at what he saw. "An old football stadium!" he exclaimed excitedly.

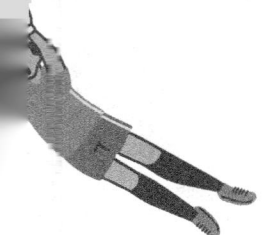

Filled with excitement, Robin called his best friends Ahmed and Luna to explore the stadium together. They took a tour through the stands and found old balls and jerseys tucked away in a small crevice next to the former substitute bench. These items were already quite wrinkled and faded. The strange names on the jerseys made Robin wonder who might have played at this place a long time ago.

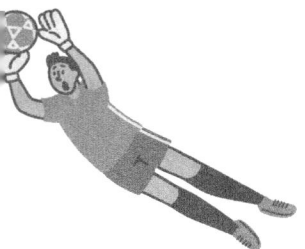

As they ventured deeper into the stadium's interior, they discovered dusty glass display cases showcasing tiny trophies and medals. Large pictures hung on the walls, featuring teams posing with wide grins. Robin scanned the faces, and suddenly, he gasped for breath — a man in one of the photos looked exactly like his grandfather!

""Oh my goodness, that's you, Grandfather John!" exclaimed Robin in astonishment. As the three friends continued their search, they found old newspaper articles in the broken display cases. And indeed, the articles confirmed that "Captain Robinho" had scored the most goals of all time for the team and led them to many championships. Robin read the proud words aloud and was filled with excitement about his ancestor's achievements.

That night, Robin could hardly sleep due to excitement. He went to his grandfather, asking him about the old times and eagerly listening to the stories. However, he learned that the man in the picture was not his grandfather but his grandfather's father, Robin's great-grandfather. With sparkling eyes, his grandfather recounted how he stood on the sidelines as his great-grandfather scored the decisive goal right there on the crumbling field where Robin stood today.

Robin was inspired by his grandfather's 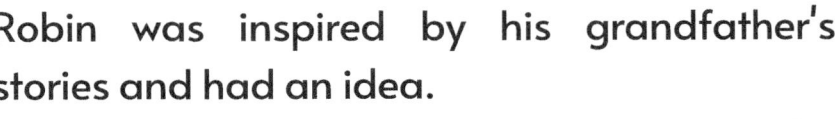 stories and had an idea.

The next day, Robin decided to renovate the dilapidated stadium and bring it back to life. He told Ahmed and Luna about his plan, and they were immediately excited. Together, they devised plans on how to restore the playing field, clean the stands, and beautify the stadium with fresh paint.

With great enthusiasm and support from their families and the community, the three friends began the renovation work. They cleared the weeds, repaired the damaged fences, set up new goals, replanted the grass, and painted the stands in the colors of their great-grandfather's team.

Slowly but surely, the stadium began to shine in new splendor. Robin, Ahmed, and Luna were proud of what they had accomplished. They invited their friends and neighbors to an opening match, where the renovated stadium was inaugurated.

Children, parents, grandparents, friends, and acquaintances formed their own teams and played with great enthusiasm on the freshly restored field. The spectators cheered and cheered on the players. There was a fantastic atmosphere, and everyone had fun playing football.

The newly radiant stadium became a place of joy and community. Over time, more and more children and adults came to play football together and discover the history of the stadium.

Robin, Ahmed, and Luna had learned an important lesson: with cooperation, enthusiasm, and support, one can achieve great things. The renovated stadium was not only a tribute to their great-grandfather John but also a place where a new generation could discover the joy of playing football, just as it was a hundred years ago.

Juan the little street footballer

Ten-year-old Juan loved football more than anything else in the whole world. Every day, he practiced his tricks on the dusty streets of his neighborhood in Buenos Aires. While the other kids played on fancy teams, Juan had his own style of playing.

He could juggle the ball so skillfully that it never touched the ground. Juan could dribble the ball through passing crowds of people and shoot it through old tire swings as if they were goals. Everyone in the neighborhood admired his impressive skills.

One sunny afternoon, a man named Edwin was passing by and saw Juan playing. Edwin was a talent scout who was on the lookout for promising young players. "Why aren't you at the team selection trials?" Edwin asked, astonished.

Juan shrugged and replied, "I prefer to play in my own way. I enjoy perfecting my tricks and having fun." Edwin was fascinated by Juan's passion and talent, realizing that he had something special.

Edwin convinced Juan to follow him and took him to a big stadium where the best youth league players trained. There, Juan saw them playing in strict formations, passing the ball among themselves. Juan knew he could change the game.

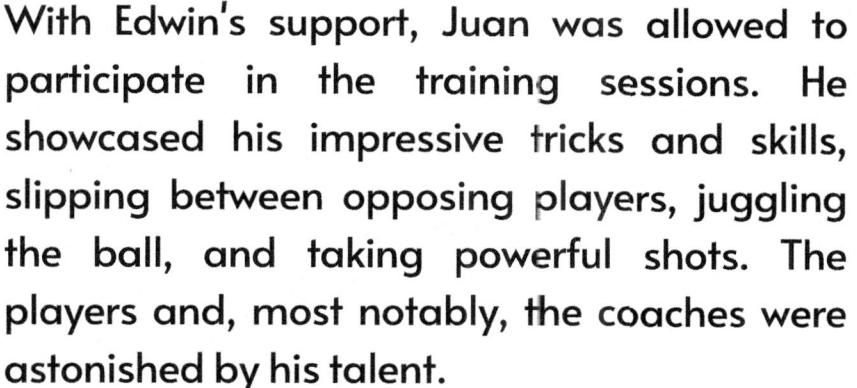

With Edwin's support, Juan was allowed to participate in the training sessions. He showcased his impressive tricks and skills, slipping between opposing players, juggling the ball, and taking powerful shots. The players and, most notably, the coaches were astonished by his talent.

Soon, the top teams heard about Juan's extraordinary abilities, and everyone wanted him in their team. However, Juan had a different idea. He decided to be part of Edwin's small neighborhood team.

Because Juan had little desire to have his creativity coached out of him. Edwin promised him that he would let him play completely freely, just the way he wanted. Juan and his team soon competed against the best teams in the region. Although they didn't have as much money or fame as the other perfectly trained teams, they showed that creativity and love for the game are just as important.

From then on, Juan thrilled the audience at every game with his tricks and captivating style of play. He demonstrated that football could also be decided by individual actions. As long as he had a ball and played with passion and enjoyment, he could achieve anything.

Juan and his team won game after game, becoming the strongest team in the region. They proved that true talent comes from within and that it doesn't always require perfectly trained team players to win.

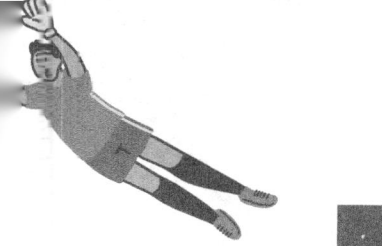

Juan's story became known throughout the neighborhood and inspired many children to start playing football and pursue their own dreams. Juan became a role model for young footballers, reminding them to find their own style of playing and pursue their passion.

And so, Juan lived happily and continued to play football with all his creativity, joy, and magic. He never played for a big club or earned a lot of money, but he entered the history books as the greatest footballer in the city.

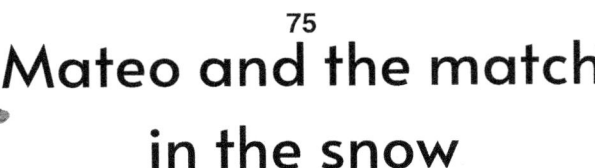

Mateo and the match in the snow

Mateo lived in a hot desert. The sun always shone hot and strong, and the sand crunched under his shoes. He was a passionate football player and played beach football at the beach with his club.

But this weekend, Mateo had the exciting opportunity to play on a proper grass field as his football club embarked on a bus trip to the high mountains of the north.

When they reached the new field, Mateo was fascinated by the lush green of the grass. It felt soft and bouncy under his feet, unlike the hard sand he was accustomed to. He couldn't wait to dribble the ball across the smooth grass.

As they warmed up, they noticed dark clouds gathering in the sky. The wind grew stronger and cooler, and suddenly, a heavy downpour began. Raindrops splashed onto the grass, forming small puddles. Mateo was initially worried that the game might be canceled, but Coach Diego laughed and said, "The best games happen during storms!"

Mateo put on his cleats and felt the wet grass enveloping his soles. When the game began, he initially found it challenging to navigate the slippery surface. However, he soon realized that the wet ground provided perfect traction for his shoes. He could run faster, stop abruptly, and shoot better.

The rain incessantly poured down on the players, but Mateo suddenly didn't mind it anymore. He enjoyed the refreshing feeling of the droplets on his skin and the splashing of the puddles as he ran through them. Sometimes, the water would splash high and wet his legs, which made him laugh.

During the game, there was a loud thunderclap that startled Mateo. But his friend Jam shouted, "That means the other team is more afraid than we are!" Mateo felt braver after hearing that.

He dribbled the ball like a slithering snake through the opponents. The wet grass facilitated his movements, and he could easily control the game. Suddenly, he took a run-up and shot the ball with full force into the wet net. A loud cheer escaped him, and his teammates slapped him on the shoulder.

They all laughed and danced in the pouring rain. Water dripped from their faces as they beamed with joy. Mateo felt the rain quenching his thirst when he stuck out his tongue, giving him energy. He realized that games in the rain can be just as fun as in sunshine.

Months later, Mateo and his team were invited back to the north, where it was now winter. There, Mateo experienced snow for the first time. Fluffy white flakes fell from the sky and covered the ground. He was fascinated by the coldness and softness of the snow. Mateo called his friends Juan and Anna over, and they ran out to explore the winter wonderland.

The snow crunched under their shoes as they ran across the field. Mateo stuck out his tongue and caught the snowflakes, which melted on his skin. He started kicking the snow around and running across the field. Sometimes, he slipped and fell into the soft snow, laughing out loud.

Mateo and his friends realized that playing in the snow was a completely new experience.

The snow changed the way the ball moved, and they adjusted their style of play. They dribbled more cautiously to avoid slipping and passed the ball more gently to maintain control.

Eventually, nobody focused on the football game anymore. The children even built a snowman together on the field and started throwing snowballs at each other. Mateo noticed that he felt very happy and alive. Despite the cold, he had a great time with all the players on the field.

Mateo felt the snow cooling his hands and coloring his cheeks rosy. He was impressed by the silence that came with the snow. Everything around him seemed muffled and peaceful as the two football teams romped across the snow-covered field.

They all built a snow tunnel together and slid down it. Mateo felt the rush of adrenaline as he sped down the hill at high speed. The snow splashed around him, and he could feel the tingling of the icy cold on his skin. It was a completely new sensation for him.

As they finally made their way home, exhausted and happy, Mateo realized that playing football is not just about the location or the weather. It's about spending time with his teammates, having fun, and experiencing new adventures.

Origin doesn't matter

Ferdinand had to leave his home and embark on a long journey to find safety. Now, he was living in a large refugee camp. But all he wished for was to play football again.

One day, Ferdinand saw a few new children kicking a ball in the camp and had a brilliant idea. "Let's start our own team!" he exclaimed excitedly. Soon, he found boys and girls from different rooms in the camp who wanted to join in.

They started practicing every day on the empty field. They taught each other tricks and how to pass the ball to their teammates. They built goals out of sticks and set up a dribbling course using old cans. Ferdinand was so skilled at dribbling that the other children called him the "King of Dribbling."

One day, a man named Gerd, around 40 years old, passed by and saw how diligently the children were training. He was a football coach and wanted to help them. Coach Gerd had several training equipment in his garage from earlier times, and he made them available to the team. He also helped the team register for a football tournament in the nearby city.

They trained hard and learned to play as a team, even though they didn't have uniforms. There were some truly talented individuals in the team.

Before the start of the tournament, Gerd got everyone the same shirts, which they painted in colorful designs and wrote their numbers and names on. In their first game, Ferdinand's team quickly fell behind. The opposing team scored a goal. However, Ferdinand's teammates didn't give up. They ran like wild animals and supported each other on the field. They cheered each other on, shouting, "We can do this if we stick together!"

Finally, Mervo got the ball and curled a beautiful banana cross into the penalty area. Ferdinand jumped high and headed the ball into the goal - their first goal! The crowd initially cheered just as loudly for Ferdinand's team as they did for the other teams. However, shortly afterward, the people in the stadium learned through the announcer that the players had undertaken a long journey to be there. They were impressed by their courage and strength.

In their second game, they faced a strong team. The opponents were big and fast, but Ferdinand's team refused to be intimidated. They had learned to work as a team and support each other. The game was fiercely contested, but towards the end of the second half, Odobert managed to score a bicycle kick goal. The stadium erupted with excitement! Ferdinand's team had won and was cheered on by the spectators.

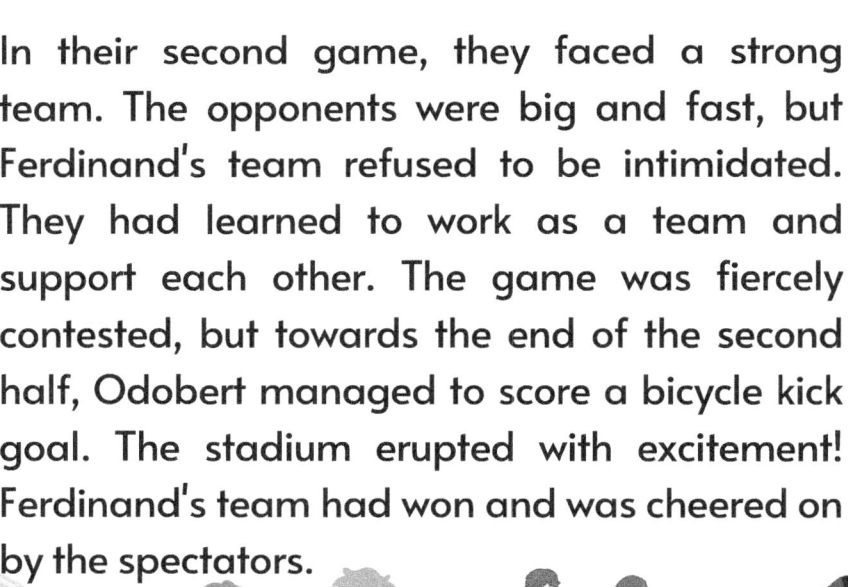

In the quarterfinals, they faced a team from the neighborhood known for their strong defense. The opponents were excellent football players, but Ferdinand and his comrades were not ready to give up. They played with all their passion and had the audience on their side.

During the game, they not only showcased their football skills but also their joy for the game. Ferdinand did a funny dance after scoring a goal, and his teammates celebrated with him. The audience laughed and applauded them.

In the end, Ferdinand's team won the quarterfinal with a score of 1:0. The crowd was ecstatic with joy and admired the players for their fighting spirit and likability. After the victory, the whole team performed a dance in front of the spectators as a thank-you for their support. The audience loved the gesture, and the team became a favorite among the fans.

In the semifinals, they faced a team that seemed unbeatable until then. The game was fiercely contested, but Ferdinand's team didn't give up. They fought until the end and were just one step away from winning the game.

Despite all their efforts, they narrowly lost the semifinal in the end. However, the audience was impressed by their performance and team spirit. They were celebrated as the "heartwarming winners" and received standing ovations and a wave of applause from the spectators.

Although they didn't win the tournament, Ferdinand's team was incredibly proud of what they had achieved. They had shown that with unity, courage, and a love for the game, great things can be accomplished.

At the end of the tournament, they were honored with a special award: the Fair Play Award. This recognition was given to them because they not only displayed great football skills but also consistently demonstrated fair and respectful behavior towards each other and the opposing teams.

Ferdinand and his friends were overjoyed. They had not only gained the respect and support of the audience but also formed new friendships. The tournament had shown them that despite difficult times and challenges, they can always stick together and be strong as a team.

A journey into the past

Adam loved exploring the old, decaying, creaky school building near his house. It was an exciting place with many mysterious nooks and crannies. On a sunny day, Adam took his football ball and went there to explore areas he had never been to before.

He kicked his ball along the dusty corridors, admiring the old structure. But suddenly, something strange happened. The ball rolled into a closet and disappeared! Adam couldn't believe it and called out, "Helloooo? Is anyone there?"

Carefully, he sneaked into the closet and was surprised to see a swirling hole right where his ball had been. Without much thought, Adam jumped through it and suddenly found himself in a magical place.

He stood on a radiant green football field, surrounded by famous football players and former legends. It was as if he had traveled to another time! A loud voice echoed and said, "Welcome to the Football Time Travel School!"

Adam could hardly believe his luck. He watched as the great Brazilian football idol Pelé sped past defenders with breathtaking speed and unleashed incredible shots on goal. It was as if his legs were acting like lightning and thunder! Adam was fascinated by Pelé's abilities.

Later, Adam encountered Lionel Messi, a small and agile wizard with the ball from Argentina. Adam suddenly wore a jersey with the number 10 and tried to catch Messi, but he was so fast and skillful that it was difficult to read his movements as he always seemed to be one step ahead. Then, Messi took Adam by the hand and gave him an important tip: "Be unpredictable! Use tricks and deceive your opponent to surprise them. Always do what they least expect."

Every new hour, a different football legend would appear and take care of Adam. Ronaldo from Portugal taught Adam how to shoot precisely and jump high to score incredible headers. Ronaldinho showed him smooth dance moves that could confuse his opponents and how to dribble through the middle between two defenders. Maradona from Argentina also shared his wisdom and helped Adam understand how to execute dribbles over long distances, bypassing the entire opposing team, to become an even better player.

Adam enjoyed every minute at the Football Time Travel School. He had the opportunity to learn from the greatest players of all time and admire their skills. But he also knew that his time there was limited, and he would soon have to return home.

A few minutes later, the shimmering hole on the football field opened once again, and Adam knew it was time to return. He said goodbye to his new friends, but he carried the memories of the football legends and their lessons in his heart.

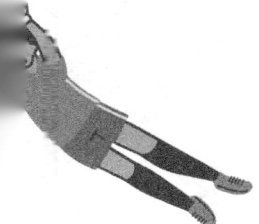

Before Adam knew it, he woke up and found himself bewildered inside the empty closet in the old school.

Adam took a few steps and played with his football ball in the nearby park. Yet, he felt different than before. He now had the knowledge and techniques of the football legends within him, and he approached the ball in a completely new way. With every shot, he thought of Ronaldo's tips, during dribbles, he channeled Messi's unpredictability, and he emulated Maradona's unmatched runs through opponents like slalom poles.

Adam knew that through his experiences, he had taken a huge leap in his performance. He now hoped for an opportunity to play a significantly larger role in his team than before. Until now, he had mostly been sitting on the bench and playing only a few minutes. He had built up an incredibly vast knowledge of how to become a better football player in many aspects. And he promised himself that he would pass on his knowledge and skills to the other children in his team.

Although the Football Time Travel School was only a dream, Adam had learned that in football, anything is possible, regardless of how much talent one has. Anyone can work hard and learn from the best. He knew that he would always remember the lessons from the football legends as he now played on the green grass, pursuing his own football dreams.

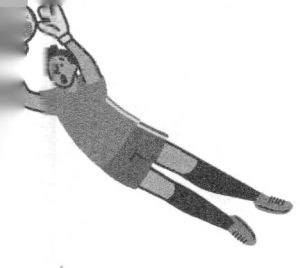

The little football blog

Finn, Max, and Luca loved playing football in their neighborhood. They were part of a small football team and had a lot of fun on the field. But one day, Finn had an idea - he wanted to share their enthusiasm for football with others.

"We could create a blog to report on our games and interview players!" Finn suggested. His friends were thrilled and got down to writing their first blog post.

They told the story of an exciting game that ended in a 2-2 draw. They described the goals that were scored and how thrilling it was to watch the game. They put a lot of effort and enthusiasm into their post. When they finished, they were satisfied and hoped to attract a few readers.

At the beginning, the only readers were their mothers, who joyfully read the blog. They were proud of their boys and encouraged them to keep going. However, the friends wanted to reach more readers and started sharing their articles on social media.

The first few articles didn't attract much attention. Only a few people knew about their blog, and the number of readers remained low. But the friends didn't get discouraged. They continued to work hard, and their content gradually improved.

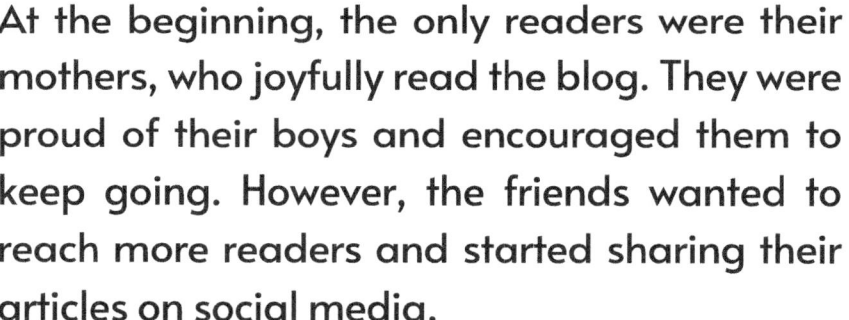

Furthermore, the three of them wanted to make their blog posts more interesting and diverse. They started conducting interviews with players from other teams to capture different perspectives and added photos and drawings to make their articles more vibrant.

With each new article, their writing and design skills improved. They conducted thorough research to provide well-researched infor- mation and carefully checked their articles for errors. As a result, the quality of their blog steadily increased.

Slowly but surely, they began to attract more readers. Other children from their school and neighborhood discovered the blog and enjoyed reading about the games and player interviews. Finn, Max, and Luca were very happy that their hard work was finally getting the attention it deserved.

With the growing readership, the friends became more motivated than ever. They worked hard to deliver interesting content and to excite their readers with thrilling stories. They wrote about every single goal and every exciting minute of the games, sharing their passion for football with others.

The football friends had succeeded! Word spread about their blog, and more and more children began reading and following their articles. They received comments and messages from their readers, thanking them for their work and asking for more content. Soon, they reached their 10,000th reader and celebrated this milestone.

To further increase their reach, they began promoting their blog on other platforms. They created their own YouTube channel and uploaded videos on TikTok, where they talked about their games and showcased highlights. This helped them reach a larger audience and attract more readers to their blog. At the same time, they built a large community of viewers for their videos, which soon garnered several thousand views per video.

In the videos, they showed game scenes in slow motion to make the small details and techniques visible. Subscribers loved seeing their favorite players in action and learning from them and the tips they provided on their channels.

Soon, the blog became so well-known that they started receiving offers, and the three friends were able to earn money through advertising as well.

The popularity of the friends continued to grow until they were even invited to major football matches. They traveled to exciting tournaments and championships, reporting on them in their blog and videos. They conducted interviews with famous players and had the privilege of being close to the field, speaking with players and coaches of big clubs before and after the games. Through their channels, the three friends now shared the magic of football with fans all around the world.

The small group proved that passion, storytelling, and football can bring people together. Though they started small, their contributions and enthusiasm later spread joy and excitement for football worldwide. This demonstrates that anyone, no matter how young or small, can share and inspire others with the world of football.

The perfect team captain

Liam was a small boy who wasn't the fastest or strongest player, but Coach Peter recognized something special in him – his enormous heart, his talent for motivating others, and the immense respect everyone seemed to have for him! That's why, at just 9 years old, Liam was appointed as the captain of the Tigers football team.

However, some older boys still laughed at the idea of little Liam being their leader. But Liam didn't let it discourage him. Every night, he studied plays to help his teammates. He dreamt of leading the way on the field and guiding his team to victory.

Then, the day arrived. Before their first game, the players gathered in a team huddle to discuss their strategy. Liam spoke with such passion that it stirred butterflies in everyone's stomachs. "Together, we will roar!" he exclaimed, full of conviction.

In their first major game, things didn't go well for the Tigers. They were trailing 2-0 at halftime! But Liam refused to be discouraged. "The game is not over yet. If we work together and play as a team, we can turn this around!" he encouraged his teammates.

In the second half, inspired by Liam's words, the Tigers fought harder than ever before. Liam passed the ball to Justin, who scored the first goal for their team! The atmosphere instantly improved, and everyone was motivated, with Liam leading the way. It seemed like the opponents bounced off him in every duel, and he persevered until he could pass to a better-positioned teammate. Defensively, he won every ball, and no opponent seemed able to get past him anymore.

The Tigers could feel the tides turning. They were filled with energy and determination. Liam cheered on his teammates, encouraging them to keep giving their best. Every player poured their heart and soul into the team.

The game grew more intense as the Tigers scored their second goal. This time, it was Liam himself who found the back of the net! The spectators erupted in cheers, and the Tigers were filled with joy. They had equalized!

Time flew by, and the game approached its end. The Tigers were determined to secure the victory. Liam orchestrated the game with clever passes and instructions. He brought out the best in every player, ensuring they worked together and marched forward.

Suddenly, there was a gap in the opposing team's defense. Liam recognized the opportunity and passed the ball to Sandro, who scored the third goal for the Tigers with a powerful shot! A loud cheer filled the stadium. The Tigers were leading for the first time in this game!

The remaining game time was fiercely contested, and the Tigers threw themselves into every duel with determination. They defended their goal with everything they had, blocking the opponent's attacks with their legs, headers, and bodies. Every player was willing to give it their all to secure the victory.

When the final whistle finally sounded, the joy was immense. Liam held the winner's trophy high, while all the Tigers ran towards him in excitement, lifting him into the air. They had turned the game around and won!

From that day on, the team and even the older players followed Liam's leadership without laughter and with great respect. He had shown that the unity of the team relies on the heart and belief of a captain. These abilities allowed Liam to transfer his will onto the entire team and surpass himself.